# Mr. Revere and I

by
Robert Lawson

## Teacher Guide

Written by
Rebecca L. Berry and Anne Troy

**Note**
The Little, Brown and Company paperback edition of the book was used to prepare this teacher guide. The page references may differ in the hardcover or other paperback editions.

---

**ISBN 1-56137-276-5**
**Copyright infringement is a violation of Federal Law.**

© 1998, 2004 by Novel Units, Inc., Bulverde, Texas. All rights reserved. No part of this publication may be reproduced, translated, stored in a retrieval system, or transmitted in any way or by any means (electronic, mechanical, photocopying, recording, or otherwise) without prior written permission from Novel Units, Inc.

Photocopying of student worksheets by a classroom teacher at a non-profit school who has purchased this publication for his/her own class is permissible. Reproduction of any part of this publication for an entire school or for a school system, by for-profit institutions and tutoring centers, or for commercial sale is strictly prohibited.

Novel Units is a registered trademark of Novel Units, Inc.  Printed in the United States of America.

To order, contact your local school supply store, or—
**Novel Units, Inc.**
P.O. Box 97
Bulverde, TX 78163-0097

**Web site: www.educyberstor.com**

Lori Mammen, Editorial Director
Suzanne K. Mammen, Curriculum Specialist
Andrea M. Harris, Production Manager/Production Specialist
Heather Johnson, Product Development Specialist
Jill Reed, Product Development Specialist
Nancy Smith, Product Development Specialist
Adrienne Speer, Production Specialist

# Table of Contents

# Skills and Strategies

**Thinking**
   Research, visualization,
   brainstorming, mapping

**Comprehension**
   Predicting, comparison/
   contrast, inference, cause
   and effect

**Writing**
   Reading response journal,
   report writing, letters
   Discussion, debate

**Vocabulary**

Context clues, word sort

**Listening/Speaking**
   Discussion, debate,
   interviewing

**Literary Elements**
   Historical fiction, table of
   contents, point of view,
   story elements, setting,
   characterization

## Summary

This is the story of the events immediately preceding the American Revolution as told by Paul Revere's horse, Scheherazade. "Sherry," once a loyal member of the King's army but destined for the glue factory, is saved by Sam Adams and enlisted by Paul Revere. Sherry becomes a true patriot and, with her most important ride, helps the Sons of Liberty to victory. Some of the events include the tea tax and the Boston Tea Party.

## Introductory Information and Activities

### Instructions Prior to Reading:

You may wish to choose one or more of the following pre-reading discussion questions/ activities. Each is designed to help students draw from their store of background knowledge about the events and themes they will meet in the story they are about to read.

### Pre-reading Discussion Questions:

1.  On Patriotism: The characters in this story displayed a high degree of patriotism. Brainstorm ways that patriotism can be shown in the following situations:

    •The pledge is being recited at a sporting event.
    •Young men and women volunteer for the National Guard.
    •People do not bother to vote on Election Day.
    •People criticize government leaders, but do not tell the leaders what they want by writing to them.

2.  On Loyalty: How do you show loyalty? Who do you expect to be loyal? Are there times when it is all right to be disloyal? How do you make such a decision?

3.  On Other Books by the Author: Have you read any other books by Robert Lawson? What were they like? What do many of his books have in common?

### Pre-reading Activities:

1.  Literary Analysis: *Mr. Revere and I* is an example of historical fiction. In historical fiction, the main characters are usually creations of the writer's imagination (although real people may be mentioned in the story). The setting is real—usually a time and place which had historical importance.

    Help students fill in the chart on the next page, comparing and contrasting historical fiction with history.

|  | HISTORICAL FICTION | HISTORY (FACTUAL) |
|---|---|---|
| Setting: | Our world | Our world |
| Characters: | May or may not be people who really lived | People who really lived |
| Action: | Could have happened but not entirely true story | True story |
| Problem: | Could have belonged to someone living at the time of the story | Real problem |
| Examples: | *My Brother Sam Is Dead* (Collier) and *Johnny Tremain* (Forbes) | *Hiroshima* (Hersey) and *Dawn* (Wiesel) |

2. Bulletin Board Ideas:
   a) Direct students to library resource books which provide short biographies of authors who write for young people. Have students then create a bulletin board/table display about Robert Lawson. On the bulletin board might go a picture of Lawson, a brief biography, and illustrated summaries of his books. The books themselves, or cigar box dioramas representing the books, could be displayed on the table below the bulletin board.

   b) Have students make or find pictures illustrating their interpretations of "life, liberty, and the pursuit of happiness." The pictures will be arranged around these words on the bulletin board.

   c) The students will make a time line of events from 1768–1776.

## Recommended Procedure for Reading this Book:
This book will be read one section at a time, using DRTA (Directed Reading Thinking Activity) Method. This technique involves reading a section, predicting what will happen next (making good guesses) based on what has already occurred in the story. (See pp. 5–6 in this guide.)

## Using Predictions in the Novel Unit Approach

We all make predictions as we read—little guesses about what will happen next, how the conflict will be resolved, which details given by the author will be important to the plot, which details will help to fill in our sense of a character. Students should be encouraged to predict, to make sensible guesses. As students work on predictions, these discussion questions can be used to guide them: What are some of the ways to predict? What is the process of a sophisticated reader's thinking and predicting? What clues does an author give us to help us in making our predictions? Why are some predictions more likely than others?

A predicting chart is included for students to record their predictions. As each subsequent chapter is discussed, you can review and correct previous predictions. This procedure serves to focus on predictions and to review the stories.

Use the facts and ideas the author gives.

Use your own knowledge.

Use new information that may cause you to change your mind.

Predictions:

_____

_____

_____

_____

## Prediction Chart

| What characters have we met so far? | What is the conflict in the story | What are your predictions? | Why did you make those predictions? |
|---|---|---|---|
| | | | |

**Initiating Activities:**

1. Look at the cover of this novel. Can you find any clues about the story? the characters?

2. Read the title page.

## "Mr. Revere and I

*Being an Account of certain
Episodes in the Career of*
**PAUL REVERE,** *Esq.*

*as recently revealed by his Horse,*
**SCHEHERAZADE,**
*late Pride of his Royal Majesty's
14th Regiment of Foot*
\* \* \* \* \* \* \* \*
*Set down and Embellished with
Numerous Drawings by*
**ROBERT LAWSON"**
\* \* \* \* \* \* \* \*

How would you say all this in the 1990s? The capitalization does not follow our rules. Why do you think the author did this?

3. Review the Table of Contents. Ask the students to choose a chapter title that interests them and to write a brief summary predicting what might happen in that chapter. Place the summaries on the bulletin board on the day before the chapter is read. Students will enjoy reading what others have predicted.

4. Post a city map of Boston and a larger map showing the surrounding cities.

5. Literary Analysis: Point of View—Writers can tell their stories from many points of view. Sometimes a central character in the story tells the story. Sometimes the storyteller is a minor character. Sometimes the storyteller is a narrator who can see inside the characters. And sometimes the writer shifts the point of view from one person to another. Looking at the title page who do you think tells most of the story of *Mr. Revere and I*?

6. Many stories have the same parts—a setting, a problem, a goal, and a series of events that lead to an ending or conclusion. These story elements may be placed on a story map. Just as a road map helps a driver get from one place to another, so too, a story map helps the reader to understand the direction of the story. There are many different types of story maps. Students may use the one included or make up their own. (See page 9 of this guide.)

We need answers to some questions which we'll look for as we begin the novel:

   •Who is the main character?
   •Where does the story take place?
   •What is the problem?

As the story is read, more characters may be added, and the setting and problem may change. After each chapter is read, changes should be made on the map.

# Story Map

Setting

Problem

Goal

Episodes

Resolution

Characters _____

_____

_____

_____

Time and Place _____

_____

_____

_____

_____

Beginning ———→ Development ———→ Outcome

_____

_____

_____

_____

_____

_____

_____

_____

# Chapter 1: "Pride of the 14th" — pp. 3–10

**Vocabulary:**

| | | |
|---|---|---|
| rustic 3 | imbecile 4 | sacrilegious 4 |
| languid 4 | copious 6 | evolutions 7 |
| adroit 7 | mortified 7 | unruly 8 |
| comport 8 | hold 8 | gaols 8 |
| caroused 8 | implacable 10 | implausible 10 |
| accoutrements 10 | | |

**Discussion Questions:**

1. Who is telling the story? *(the horse, Scheherazade)* How might this change the tone of the story?

2. What type of personality does Scheherazade seem to have? *(haughty, arrogant)* How did you come to that conclusion? *(speech, word choice, attitude, perspective)* Students may read certain parts to prove their points.

3. Study the picture of Sir Barnstable on page 5. Compare with the author's description on pp. 5–6. What kind of illustration would you draw? Do you think you would like Sir Barnstable? Why or why not?

4. Characters are developed by what they say, think, and do, and by how others in the novel react to them. In this chapter, what do we learn about Scheherazade? Begin an attribute web for her. (See pp. 12–13 in this guide.)

5. Why does Scheherazade say the "Glorious" was misnamed? *(Page 8, It was a leaky, dirty ship with an awful crew.)* Can you think of another example of something that is misnamed?

6. Why was Scheherazade sent from England to Boston? *(page 8, to quell the rebel uprisings)*

**Prediction:**
What problems will this special horse face in America?

**Supplementary Activities:**

1. Research King George.

2. Invite a horse expert to discuss horse care, diet, etc.

3. Writing: Begin a journal in which you react to each section of the story you read. Reactions might include: Questions you have about the story; memories the story evokes; people or other stories of whom characters remind you; judgments about whether you agree or disagree with what characters have done; your thoughts about topics which come up—such as treatment of animals, best friends, loyalties, etc. Try sometimes including vocabulary words from the story in your journal.

## Using Character Webs—In the Novel Unit Approach

Attribute Webs are simply a visual representation of a character from the novel. They provide a systematic way for the students to organize and recap the information they have about a particular character. Attribute webs may be used after reading the novel to recapitulate information about a particular character or completed gradually as information unfolds, done individually, or finished as a group project.

One type of character attribute web uses these divisions:

- How a character acts and feels. (How does the character feel in this picture? How would you feel if this happened to you? How do you think the character feels?)

- How a character looks. (Close your eyes and picture the character. Describe him to me.)

- Where a character lives. (Where and when does the character live?)

- How others feel about the character. (How does another specific character feel about our character?)

In group discussion about the student attribute webs and specific characters, the teacher can ask for backup proof from the novel. You can also include inferential thinking.

Attribute webs need not be confined to characters. They may also be used to organize information about a concept, object or place.

## Attribute Web

The attribute web below is designed to help you gather clues the author provides about what a character is like. Fill in the blanks with words and phrases which tell how the character acts and looks, as well as what the character says and what others say about him or her.

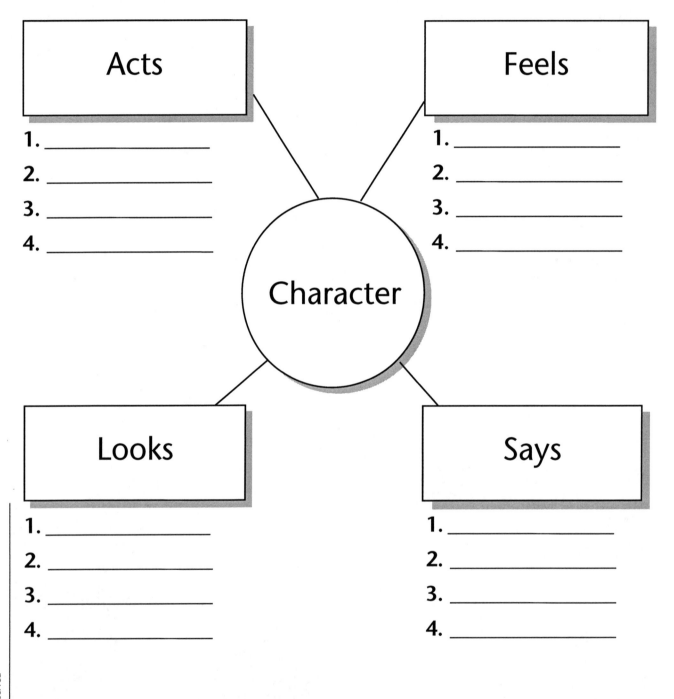

# Attribute Web

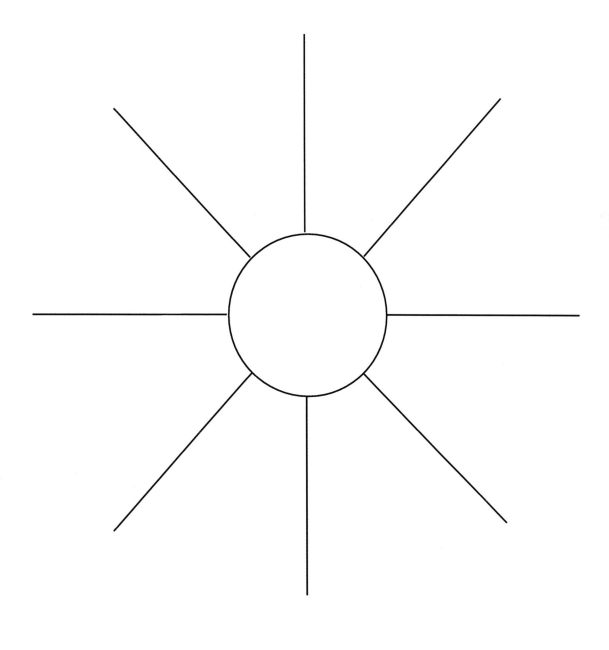

# Chapter 2: "Welcome to Boston" — pp. 11–17

**Vocabulary:**

| | | |
|---|---|---|
| ferried 12 | edible 12 | countrified 12 |
| flimsy 12 | abustle 13 | queues 14 |
| raucous 15 | crustacean 16 | hue 16 |
| absolute 16 | irresistible 16 | vittles 17 |
| yahoos 17 | churlish 17 | impudently 17 |

**Discussion Questions:**

1. How did the people of Boston react to the arrival of the British? *(pp. 14–17, They were rude, did not cheer for the British and refused to rent quarters to them.)*

2. Why do you think the townspeople were sullen? *(page 13)*

3. Start a dual list of insults used on the British *("Lobsterbacks," page 16)* and on the Americans *("clam-eating yahoos," page 17).*

**Supplementary Activity:**

Locate and mark Faneuil Hall and Boston Common on the Boston map.

# Chapter 3: "Officers, Gentlemen and Bumpkins" — pp. 18–25

**Vocabulary:**

| | | |
|---|---|---|
| missiles 19 | stanch 19 | foul 19 |
| exorbitant 19 | disbursements 19 | desolate 19 |
| mangled 20 | marauders 20 | ventured 21 |
| profusely 21 | emerged 22 | hibernation 22 |
| malcontents 23 | defaced 25 | notoriously 25 |

**Discussion Questions:**

1. Why was the King's Arms Tavern renamed the Liberty Belle? *(Page 19, The soldiers of the King were staying there, and the Patriots, to show their displeasure, threw oyster shells, fish heads and other unpleasant missiles at the inn and its windows. The owner, although a Loyalist and supporter of the King, renamed his inn the Liberty Belle to make the Patriots think he favored their cause and to stop the damage of his inn.)*

2. How did the British soldiers spend their first winter in America? *(page 21, eating, playing cards, and sleeping)*

3. How did the townspeople treat the soldiers? Why? *(Page 22, The townspeople tried to ignore the soldiers who were a threat to the way of life they wanted; Page 25, Sometimes the Patriots showed their displeasure by causing disorder.)*

**Prediction:**
What trouble could Barnstable bring on himself and his horse by his bad card playing?

**Supplementary Activity:**
Begin a series of **"Who's Who?"** posters for people who influenced the American Revolution. These posters may include pictures and biographical information.

## Chapter 4: "Pride Goeth before . . ." — pp. 26–34

**Vocabulary:**

| | | |
|---|---|---|
| steeplechase course 26 | wagered 27 | prodigious 27 |
| rebellious 28 | impudence 28 | preposterous 28 |
| demagogue 28 | gala 29 | calamity 29 |
| reprobate 30 | vicious 31 | shied 31 |
| pandemonium 32 | arrogant 32 | contempt 32 |
| hostelry 33 | ruffianly 33 | unsavory 33 |

**Discussion Questions:**

1.  How does Sherry see the Sons of Liberty? *(Page 28, They were low class people, with little money, who were rebellious.)* What did Sherry think of Sam Adams? *(Page 28, He was a loud-mouth instigator.)*

2.  What did the townspeople think of racing? Why would they especially disapprove of this recreation on Sunday? *(pp. 26–27)*

3.  Describe Sherry's racing accident. *(pp. 30–32, Sherry stumbled during the race when a colonist distracted her by throwing a shell at her.)*

4.  Why was it such a disaster that Sherry lost the race? *(Page 29, It was "nothing short of a calamity" to her officer, Sir Cedric, because he had so many debts, I.O.U.'s to pay off.)*

5.  Why does Sherry get a new owner, Stinky Nat? *(Page 33, Barnstable has to settle his debts using Sherry as payment.)*

6.  What does the title of this chapter refer to? What do you think it means? *(Sherry is a very proud horse and because of the gambling of her master, she will be reduced to poverty and abuse.)*

**Prediction:**
How will life change for Sherry with Stinky Nat as her master?

**Supplementary Activities:**
1. Use a T-Diagram to compare and contrast Sherry and Ajax. Continue to add to this diagram as the novel is read.

| SHERRY | AJAX |
|---|---|
| | |

Physical Attributes:

Temperament:

2. Begin a list of Paul Revere's occupations. Continue to add to this list throughout the story. Eventually use this list to create a resume for Revere.

3. Create a button with a slogan reflecting a group to whom you are loyal. Share reasons for loyalty to this particular group.

4. If the Sons of Liberty were to have a party, what might the purpose and the theme be? Design an invitation to their party.

5. Research the Sons of Liberty and Sam Adams.

6. Hold a debate on the pros and cons of gambling.

## Chapter 5: "Less than the Dust" — pp. 35–46

### Vocabulary:

| | | |
|---|---|---|
| ramshackle 35 | stench 35 | profanity 36 |
| offal 36 | attainments 36 | unsavory 37 |
| atrocious 38 | inevitable 38 | gurry 38 |
| wain 39 | farrier 39 | arrogant 39 |
| callous 39 | equine 39 | expropriated 41 |
| bedizened 42 | popinjay 42 | catcalls 43 |
| disillusionment 43 | covey 44 | steed 44 |
| warily 45 | posterity 45 | |

### Discussion Questions:

1. What does Hezzy mean when he says Nat is not good at dice, but "they was his dice"? *(page 36)* What are the implications of this statement? *(Nat cheated; therefore, Sherry does not legally belong to him.)*

2. Why didn't Sherry rebel against such an unseemly way of life at the glue factory? *(Page 36, She had no strength or spirit due to her poor physical/mental condition.)*

3. What does it mean to "break someone's spirit"?

4. Have you ever tried to hide from someone due to embarrassment like Sherry tried to avoid Ajax? Describe. What forces such irrational action? *(page 38)*

5. How and why does Sam Adams arrange the transfer of Sherry from Stinky Nat to Paul Revere? Do you think that was legal? Defend you answers. *(pp. 39–41)*

6. Sam Adams said, "Paul Revere needs a horse badly for his duties; you all know what *they* are." *(page 40)* Why did the author italicize the word "they"? *(preparation for the war against the King and England)* What do you know about Paul Revere's Ride?

7. There are many little jokes in this novel. Explain why these statements might be funny.

   " 'Who's paying for it?' the other countered warily. 'Not you, I hope?'
   'Posterity,' Sam answered grandly.
   'Don't know's I've ever heard the name,' said Ebenezer, 'but I'll take a chance on him.' " *(page 45)*

   " 'She'd better have two-three weeks' rest though.'
   'She'll have to,' Paul Revere laughed. 'You see, I've never yet been on a horse.' " *(page 46)*

8. Why do you think many people volunteered to help Paul Revere get settled with Sherry?

**Prediction:**
How will Sherry manage with a new master who does not know how to ride a horse? What new indignities will she suffer?

**Supplementary Activities:**
1. Brainstorm a list of adjectives and emotions reflecting Sherry's experience at the glue factory.

2. Based on Sherry's daily routine, what would you say the ingredients of glue are? (garbage, horns, hooves, etc.) Write a creative recipe for glue.

3. Research glue. What are the ingredients in glue today? How does glue differ from paste?

4. Study horse terms (mare, pony, thoroughbred, etc.).

5. Create a puzzle center to share horse puzzles. Entitle the center "Horsing Around."

# Chapter 6: "The Loving Family" — pp. 47–58

**Vocabulary:**

| | | |
|---|---|---|
| bountifully 48 | incessantly 48 | sedate 48 |
| seditious 50 | affray 50 | discreetly 50 |
| prominent 50 | sedition 51 | grimace 51 |
| welts 52 | wry 52 | caldron 52 |
| reproved 55 | traitorous 55 | desertion 55 |
| stanch 56 | hostile 56 | pathetically 56 |
| shilling 56 | incompetence 56 | |

**Discussion Questions:**
1. How did Sherry regain her self-respect? *(page 47, through the love and attention of the Revere family)*

2. How was it possible that Sherry was so involved in the daily happenings of the Revere household? *(Page 49, Sherry's stall window looked into the Revere kitchen.)*

3. Why had Giles Treadwell joined the British Army? *(Page 53, They had gotten him drunk, given him money, and pressed him into the army.)*

4. If you were Giles Treadwell, would you have left the British Army to join the Americans? Why or why not? *(pp. 51–53)*

5. What did Sam Adams mean when he said, "Every Patriot knows what Colonel Dalrymple had for breakfast before he has digested it"? *(Page 56, The Patriots were aware of all British activities.)*

6. Do you think Sherry will ever completely forsake her British loyalty? *(Page 55, "Yet I had been brought up in the firm tradition that of all military crimes desertion was the very worst. I **should** have been horrified and outraged, but I could not be. I just became more confused and upset in my mind as time passed by.")*

## Prediction:

Titles of chapters are very important. What do you think "Poor Deluded Yokels" refers to? Look at the picture on page 59. What do you think will happen?

## Supplementary Activities:

1. Design a family tree representing the entire Revere family. Include Sherry in the appropriate place.

2. Using your cumulative list of Paul Revere's jobs and talents, create a resume.

3. Locate and mark Medford on the map.

4. Investigate the artwork of a silversmith.

5. Research the Boston Massacre and design a political cartoon.

# Chapter 7: "Poor Deluded Yokels" — pp. 59–70

## Vocabulary:

| | | |
|---|---|---|
| deluded 59 | shied 60 | lash 60 |
| contempt 62 | preposterous 62 | prominent 63 |
| tuppence 63 | poop deck 64 | minions 65 |
| donned 67 | exasperation 68 | venture 69 |
| barnacles 70 | | |

## Discussion Questions:

1. Sherry seems to feel that "the clothes make the man." *(page 60)* Do you agree? Why or why not?

2. Why didn't the Sons of Liberty want the "Dartmouth" to unload its cargo in Boston? *(Page 63, They were protesting the tea tax set by England.)*

3. What bind is Mr. Rotch in? *(pp. 68–70, The Patriots refuse to let him unload the tea. He cannot sail out of the harbor without clearance papers or the British guns would blow the ships to matchwood. The Governor refuses him clearance papers. Because of port regulation, any ship docking in Boston Harbor must be unloaded within 20 days. So Mr. Rotch can neither go nor stay with his cargo of tea.)*

**Supplementary Activities:**
1. Locate and mark the surrounding areas of Newton, Weston, Lexington, Concord, Marblehead, Salem, Gloucester, Newburyport, and Portsmouth on the classroom map.

2. Research the purpose, training, duties, and importance of the Minutemen. Why were they so named?

3. Investigate the weapons and uniforms of the Revolutionary War period. How did the Patriots' uniforms differ from the British?

4. How does a musket work?

# Chapter 8: "Big Doings at Griffin's Wharf" — pp. 71–79

**Vocabulary:**

| | | |
|---|---|---|
| decisive 71 | milled 72 | rostrum 73 |
| chaise 73 | distraught 73 | throng 73 |
| emerged 75 | contingent 76 | profusely 76 |
| masqueraders 77 | concoct 77 | exulted 78 |
| stupendous 78 | conveyed 78 | flounced 79 |

**Discussion Questions:**
1. What was Mr. Revere's job? *(page 72, attend all the meetings and to keep the leaders abreast of the latest happenings)*

2. For what was Sam Adams' speech, "This meeting can do nothing more to save the country!" a signal? *(Page 73, All the Patriots were to don their costumes for the Boston Tea Party.)*

3. How did the Sons of Liberty solve Mr. Rotch's problem? *(Page 77, They unloaded Mr. Rotch's ship and solved his problem by dumping the tea in the harbor.)*

4. Why do you think the Sons of Liberty dressed like Indians?

5. Why do you think the author included the character of old Mrs. Revere? *(Page 78, She added a touch of humor to the seriousness of the Boston Tea Party.)*

## Supplementary Activities:

1. Calculate the current cost (in U.S. dollars) of the tea dumped overboard using the information on page 78 and current exchange rates in the newspaper. (Number of English pounds times exchange rate equals U.S. dollars.) Approximately 340 cases of tea were dumped. How much was each case worth?

2. Dramatize the Boston Tea Party.

3. Write a short inspirational speech that Sam Adams might have delivered. Present it with true Adams' flair.

# Chapter 9: "Revere Rides Again—and Again" — pp. 80–91

## Vocabulary:

| | | |
|---|---|---|
| tarry 81 | surliness 82 | treacherous 82 |
| miraculous 84 | tumultuous 86 | detaining 88 |
| dire 89 | calamity 90 | privation 91 |
| shoddy 91 | tarnished 91 | |

## Discussion Questions:

1. Why do you think it was important for Paul Revere to spread the news regarding the Sons of Liberty and their progress? *(page 88)*

2. Sherry was homesick during her ride to New York. Do you believe that an animal can get homesick? Have you ever been homesick? How does an animal show homesickness? a human?

3. What were three effects of the Tea Act of 1773? *(pp. 89–90, The Colonists petitioned Parliament; the Sons of Liberty organized to protest; and the Sons of Liberty dumped the tea [Boston Tea Party].)* Make a cause-effect chart. (See pp. 22–23 in this guide.)

## Supplementary Activities:

1. It took Paul five days to ride from Boston to New York. Using a map with a scale, calculate the mileage. On the average, about how many miles per day did he ride? How long does it take to cover this distance today by plane? by train? by car?

2. Write a cure for homesickness.

3. Draft a letter to King George stating the colonies' response to the closing of Boston Harbor. Write this letter with quill and ink.

4. Draw a Christmas tree surrounded by the gifts for the Revere family. What gift would you give to Sherry? Include Sherry's gift under the tree. Attach a rationale for Sherry's gift.

# Cause-Effect Chart

The chart below shows the cause of the Stamp Act. What is it? It shows two effects of the Stamp Act. What are they? Notice the way in which an effect can become a cause of the next event.

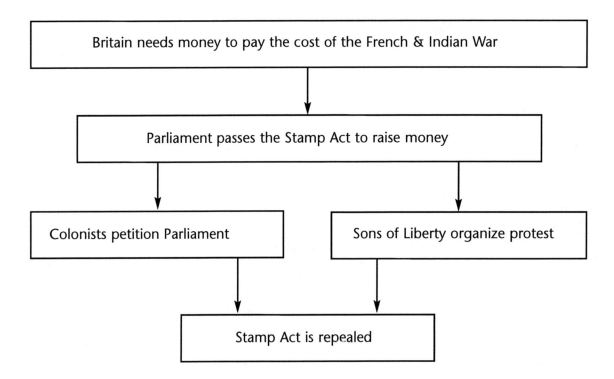

Look at this chart and think about cause ⟶ effect.

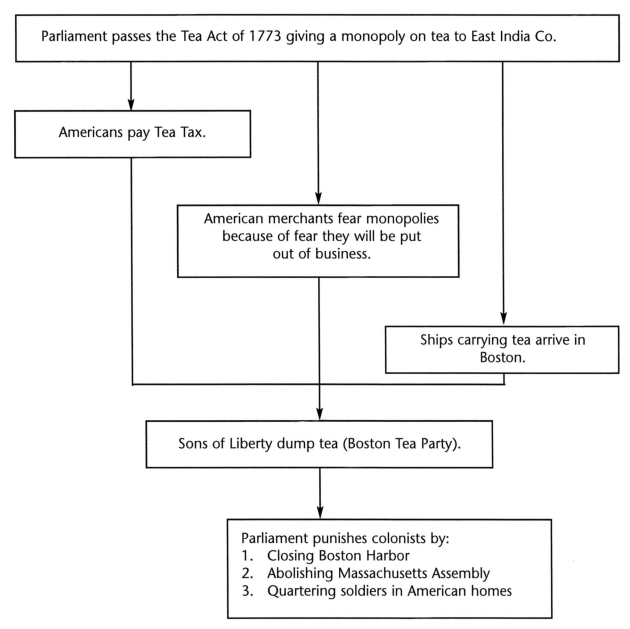

1. What were three effects of the Tea Act of 1773?

2. Why were the merchants afraid of monopolies?

3. What was the effect of the Boston Tea Party?

4. What was the cause of Massachusetts losing its assembly?

5. Why did the American colonists become angry? What was an effect of this anger?

# Chapter 10: "Closed Port" — pp. 92–106

## Vocabulary:

| | | |
|---|---|---|
| creditable 94 | convened 94 | resolutions 95 |
| alleviate 96 | transcends 97 | ingenuity 97 |
| renovation 97 | reprimands 98 | expedition 98 |
| abominable 98 | pommel 98 | manned 99 |
| magazine 100 | jollity 100 | depleted 101 |
| contemptuously 102 | monotony 102 | slithered 104 |
| exhilarated 105 | allegiance 105 | sullen 106 |

## Discussion Questions:

1. Describe Sherry's first impression of Ben Franklin and George Washington. *(Page 95, "Dr. Franklin was short and dumpy in figure and dressed somewhat like a Quaker. He did not impress me especially...General George Washington, on the other hand, was tremendously impressive...")*

2. What was the purpose of the rigorous trip to Portsmouth? *(page 98, to capture a large supply of powder and small arms guarded by only 5 British troopers and a captain)*

3. How was Sherry's second meeting with Ajax different from the previous one? *(Page 102, Sherry was not ashamed even though Ajax addressed her with derogatory names.)* Why was this a true turning point for Sherry? Prove it. *(Page 102, "Until that moment I had not fully realized how glorious it was to be free!")*

4. How did Hezekiah save Sherry's day? *(Page 103, He flipped a barrel into the middle of the lane when Ajax was chasing Sherry.)* Why did he do this?

5. Why did Paul Revere move to the outskirts of the city? *(pp. 103–105, He was in jeopardy of being caught by the British because he was becoming very well known.)*

## Prediction:

What adventures lie ahead for Sherry and her respected friend, Mr. Revere?

## Supplementary Activities:

1. Design a thank you from Washington to Paul Revere for repairing his false teeth.

2. Research the development of false teeth.

3. The writer describes the setting by telling about the sounds, sights, smells, and feeling of the place. Reread Chapter 10. Then fill in the chart by writing words and phrases from the story under each heading: See, Hear, Touch, Taste, and Smell. Use the page number.

| Page No. | See | Hear | Touch | Taste | Smell |
|---|---|---|---|---|---|
| 92 | "town now fairly crawled with red-coated soldiers" | | | | |
| 98 | | | "the puddles were all turned to ice, the ruts were frozen hard as flint" | | |
| 106 | | horses, stamping, shifting and grumbling; endless heavy pacing of sentries; gruff commands; morning drumbeat rousing us out | | | |

## Chapter 11: "Lights in the Belfry" — pp. 107–120

### Vocabulary:

| | | |
|---|---|---|
| confinement 108 | wrathful 108 | reposing 109 |
| braggart 109 | lair 113 | cravens 113 |
| ignominiously 113 | | |

### Discussion Questions:

1. What was General Gage's plan? *(page 109, take supplies from Concord and capture Hancock and Adams)*

2. How do Hancock and Adams react to Paul's first warning? *(Page 113, They did not take it too seriously.)*

3. Explain the entire plan devised to warn the Patriots of the British advance. *(Page 116, Riders arranged to warn the countryside after the signal from Old North Church.)*

4. Why do you think the author includes Mrs. Revere begging Paul not to forget her sewing basket? *(page 117)*

**Prediction:**

What could go wrong with the plan?

**Supplementary Activities:**
1. Map out the two possible routes Gage could take to accomplish his mission. Highlight the actual route.

2. Design a trunk as mentioned on page 116. Include as its contents a list of important Patriot leaders, as well as any other factual/fictional secrets that the Patriots might have kept in it.

## Chapter 12: "The Last Ride" — pp. 121–128

**Vocabulary:**

| | | |
|---|---|---|
| ominous 122 | gratifying 125 | derisive 125 |
| awry 128 | ardor 129 | disheartened 134 |
| commendations 134 | nauseating 137 | stench 137 |

**Discussion Questions:**
1. How were Sherry and Paul Revere separated? *(Page 135, They were both captured by the British. Sherry distracted the British while Paul quietly slipped away.)*

2. What advantage did Sherry have in her knowledge of the North American countryside over the British horses? *(Sherry knew what skunks were and avoided them.)* How did the skunks help Sherry to escape? *(Page 137, The Sergeant riding Sherry got off the horse to help the officers and horses overcome by the stench, and, with that, Sherry made a dash for freedom.)*

3. IIow was Sherry shot? *(Page 137, As she escaped, she was hit in the shoulder.)*

**Prediction:**

Will Sherry survive the gunshot wound?

**Supplementary Activity:**

Compare the fighting style of the British and the Americans.

# Chapter 13: "Warrior's Return" — pp. 139–149

## Vocabulary:

| | | |
|---|---|---|
| aghast 139 | idiotic 140 | caracoled 140 |
| platoons 140 | deploy 140 | arrogant 141 |
| disperse 141 | shakos 143 | haversacks 143 |
| prostrated 143 | emitted 143 | semblance 143 |
| futile 145 | delirious 147 | |

## Discussion Questions:

1. The British retreated from the Patriots in Lexington. In your opinion, is it ever honorable to retreat? Wise? Explain.

2. Why do you think the British did not win this first battle?

3. How was Sherry the first hero in the War of Independence? (*Page 149, "Sherry has suffered the first wound and shed the first blood in our War of Independence."*)

# Postscript — pp. 150–152

## Vocabulary:

| | | |
|---|---|---|
| embarking 151 | yardarm 151 | destined 151 |
| prosperous 151 | procure 152 | |

## Discussion Questions:

1. Why was March 17, 1776 important? (*Page 150, British forces left Boston.*)

2. Why do you think the author included what happened to Ajax in the conclusion? (*page 151*)

3. What did Sherry consider every bit as good as a medal from Congress for her services? (*page 152, reward of apples*)

4. Why was this a good ending for this novel?

## Culminating Activities

1. If this book were to be made into a movie, whom would you cast in what roles? Why? What night would you schedule it as a T.V. movie? Opposite what other show? Write a short blurb for the T.V. Guide.

2. Read the poem "The Midnight Ride of Paul Revere" by Longfellow. Compare it to the story. Set the poem to music/rap.

3. Choose one of Paul Revere's professions and create a "shingle" he might have had on display. Possibly include some secret code word or pictures.

4. Research the validity of the facts from the story. For example:

   • Washington's wooden teeth;
   • Sam Adams' oratory skills;
   • Hancock's handsome looks and preoccupation with the ladies;
   • Revere's lack of horse-riding experience.

5. Complete a Venn Diagram comparing Sherry at the beginning of the story to Sherry at the end of the story.

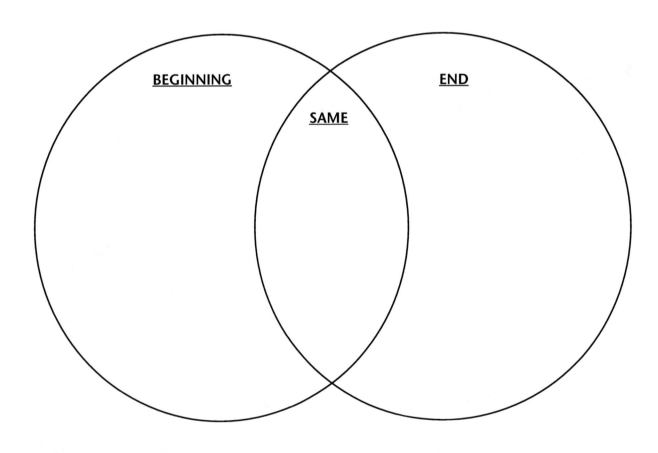

6. Read the following books on the Revolutionary War and compare the information. The class may be divided to read the three novels at the same time. (Novel Units® guides are available for both of them.)

•*Johnny Tremain* (Forbes)
•*My Brother Sam Is Dead* (Collier)

## Vocabulary Activities

1. Vocabulary Bee: The teacher (or student) gives a definition and a student supplies the word. The game is played like a spelling bee. This may be played in cooperative groups with the teacher using an answer key.

2. Related Words: Students may pick two words from the displayed lists and tell how they might be related.

   For example: mishap—exasperation. After an unfortunate accident (mishap), the workers were annoyed and angry (exasperated). (Mishap causes the exasperation.)

3. Words in Context: Ask students to "guess" at the word meaning from the context, telling why for each guess. Make a list of "why answers" to teach context clues.

4. Decide what other prefixes and suffixes may be added to vocabulary words and note how these change the word meanings.

5. Create a word search for a classmate to decode.

6. Make a large chart for a class word sort: nouns, action words, describing words—adjectives, adverbs.

7. Students will make predictions about how the author will use vocabulary to tell about the setting, characters, the problem or goal, the actions, resolution, or feeling of a character in a story.

8. Play a 20 questions-type game (pairs, groups, or whole class) where a student or the teacher selects a word for the class to identify by asking up to 20 questions (or 10 questions) about the word which may be answered by a yes, no, or sometimes answer.

9. Draw pictures to remember the word definitions.

10. Play charades to dramatize words.

# Activity Sheet

Put the letter of the word in the left column under the appropriate heading in the right column.

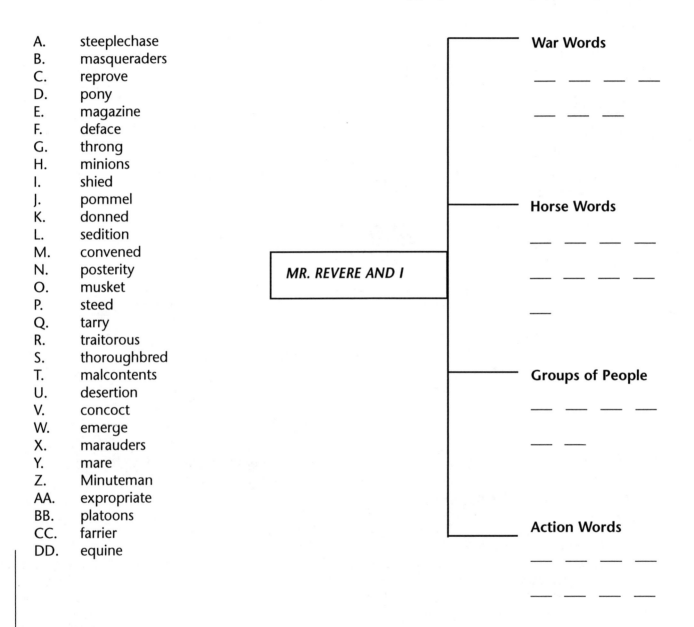

A.  steeplechase
B.  masqueraders
C.  reprove
D.  pony
E.  magazine
F.  deface
G.  throng
H.  minions
I.  shied
J.  pommel
K.  donned
L.  sedition
M.  convened
N.  posterity
O.  musket
P.  steed
Q.  tarry
R.  traitorous
S.  thoroughbred
T.  malcontents
U.  desertion
V.  concoct
W.  emerge
X.  marauders
Y.  mare
Z.  Minuteman
AA.  expropriate
BB.  platoons
CC.  farrier
DD.  equine

MR. REVERE AND I

War Words
__ __ __ __
__ __ __

Horse Words
__ __ __ __
__ __ __
__

Groups of People
__ __ __ __
__ __

Action Words
__ __ __ __
__ __ __ __

Answers: War Words—E, L, O, R, U, Z, BB; Horse Words—A, D, I, J, P, S, Y, CC, DD;
Groups of People—B, G, H, N, T, X; Action Words—C, F, K, M, Q, V, W, AA.

# Assessment for *Mr. Revere and I*

Assessment is an on-going process. The following ten items can be completed during the novel study. Once finished, the items will be checked by both the teacher and student. Points may be added to indicate the level of understanding.

Name _____ Date _____

| Student | Teacher | | |
|---------|---------|---|---|
| _____ | _____ | 1. | Create a poster to review the important elements of historical fiction. |
| _____ | _____ | 2. | Keep a predicting chart as you read the book, adding and deleting at each chapter. |
| _____ | _____ | 3. | Fill in attribute webs for Scheherazade and Paul Revere; only use information from the book. |
| _____ | _____ | 4. | Fill out a story map to review the book's plot. Attach a map to mark the book's setting. |
| _____ | _____ | 5. | Give yourself credit for each vocabulary activity you complete. (See list of suggestions on page 29.) |
| _____ | _____ | 6. | Keep a reading response journal as you read the book. (See directions on page 10.) |
| _____ | _____ | 7. | Make a list of things you could include in a portfolio for Scheherazade. Give a reason for each choice. |
| _____ | _____ | 8. | Explain cause and effect with a flow chart of events referenced in the book. |
| _____ | _____ | 9. | Choose one of the culminating activities for which to complete a written response. |
| _____ | _____ | 10. | Write a letter to the principal praising or panning the book. |

# Notes